Opus 70

Edition Axel Menges and the authors would like to thank the Latvian National Library Foundation for their help and cooperation in preparing this publication. They would also like to thank the Ministry of Culture of Latvia, the National Library of Latvia, and Hill International for their support.

Latvijas Nacionālās bibliotēkas
ATBALSTA BIEDRĪBA

Gunnar Birkerts
National Library of Latvia
Riga

Text
Jānis Dripe

Photographs
Indriķis Stūrmanis

Edition Axel Menges

Editor: Axel Menges

ISBN 978-3-932565-70-0

Printing and binding: Graspo CZ, a. s., Zlín, Czech Republic

Translation into English: Inta Liepiņa
Design: Axel Menges

Contents

Jānis Dripe

Gunnar Birkerts, National Library of Latvia, Riga

History of the design development

To understand the whole complexity of the project of the National Library of Latvia and why it took so long for the new building of the National Library to be built, we need to take a step back and look at the entire geopolitical context and developments in the history of Latvia. The idea of its construction was conceived already before WWII in the independent State of Latvia; it was cherished all through the Soviet period and then another 23 years in the re-established independent State of Latvia. The dream of a new building could not come true for nearly a century because of changing political powers, indecisiveness of politicians and officials, lack of funds and lack of an appropriate design. During this period of uncertainty, the location and the name of the National Library changed several times reflecting the changes of the ruling power in Latvia.

Soon after the proclamation of Latvia (1918) and foundation of the State Library in 1919, it became clear that a new building would be necessary for this important function. Jānis Misiņš, the first director of the Library, had no option but to use cramped spaces in the old town of Riga where the reading room could admit only 40 people. The basis of the State Library was formed by a collection of books from the library of the former Russian Theological Seminary. Already in 1921, the State Library moved to another building previously occupied by the Ministry of Education in the historic centre of Riga at Pils laukums 2. The same year an important law for the State Library was passed making it compulsory to send each copy of printed material to the library. As early as in 1928 the first serious public debate started about the necessity to store all books and facilities of the Latvian State Library in a new separate building because until then and a long time afterwards the library was scattered in several buildings adapted for its needs in Old Riga. Issue No 2 of *Ilustrētais žurnāls* (Illustrated Magazine) in 1928 stated: »The Cabinet of Ministers has brought forward the idea of building a large edifice for accommodation of the state and university library as well as other functions in order to commemorate the 10th anniversary of the Latvian State. The Budgetary Committee of the Saeima (Parliament) has decided to allocate 200,000 lats in this year's State budget for the necessary preparatory works, provided that only 10,000 lats can be used for the elaboration of the design«. Despite the efforts of Mārtiņš Stumbergs, the second director of the State Library, who was in charge for 20 years (1920–40), apart from negotiations and non-binding resolutions adopted by senior officials nothing much came out of it. At that time, the priority was given to construction of the Monument to Freedom and the building of the Court of Justice and the Ministry of Finance. In 1940, two more buildings in Old Riga, i.e. at Jēkaba iela 6/8 and Anglikāņu iela 5, were provided to the State Library. They housed the sections of the Library up to 2014 when the new building was completed.

In 1944, the political regime changed again, and the Latvian State Library became the State Library of the Latvian SSR. In 1948, there was still hope that a new library building would be built on the site where once stood the Town Hall that was partly destroyed during the war. If a political decision made in Moscow to blow up the rest of the House of Blackheads, a great architectural and cultural monument, on Town Hall Square in Riga was implemented, then despite the active participation of the library employees in removal of WWII debris, the promise to build there a new library did not materialize. In fact, the master plan developed by architects Edgars Pučiņš and Jevgēņijs Vasiļjevs intended to extend significantly the historic Kaļķu iela and to create a new city square instead of Town Hall Square. On the new city square an area was set aside also for the building of the State Library.

After Pils laukums (then already Pionieru laukums) 2 the main section of the Library was once again relocated in 1956 to Kr. Barona iela 14 where the former House of Credit and Savings Association used to be located, and part of the Library sections moved to Kr. Barona iela 3. These buildings were located outside the boundaries of the medieval old town of Riga and the city canal with its green belt of parks established in the place of Riga's fortifications that were razed between 1854 and 1856.

Interestingly, for the site where the National Library of Latvia is currently located, in 1961 a competition was held for construction of a design institute. The competition was won by Marta Staņa, a well-known Soviet modernist architect. She proposed to construct a laconic 14-storey parallelepiped designed in a modernist style with its narrow façade facing the River Daugava.

The next event was related to the state of affairs characteristic of a Soviet regime, namely, in 1971 the name of Vilis Lācis, who was a popular writer and chaired the government of the Soviet Latvia, was added to the State Library of the Latvian SSR.

In the 1960s, the idea of constructing a new library building re-emerged and in 1966 three possible sites were analyzed, including the current location of the National Library on the left riverbank of the Daugava, in Ķīversala. According to the zoning in Riga's master plan, this city block belonged to the city centre, and thus the monumental edifice of the National Library along with the hotel and office building erected nearby would have formed the central compositional element of the new development on the left riverbank of the Daugava. It has always been crucial for the building of the National Library to be located in the city centre where it would be accessible for pedestrians and by public transport.

Another oddity of the Soviet period was the fact that the Republic of Latvia could not make the final decision itself when such large objects were concerned. A set procedure required for such important buildings to be designed in institutes in Moscow or Leningrad specializing in the particular area. In 1973, the Central Institute for Scientific Research and Experimental Design of Entertainment Buildings and Sports Facilities (architects Stuzhin and Pashchenko) elaborated a technical design for the Library that, miraculously, was rejected in Riga. Already in 1975 the Soviet government of Latvia commissioned a sketch of the Library building from the institute Pilsētprojekts (then Latgiprogorstroj). The management of the institute entrusted the leading Latvian architect Modris Ģelzis (1929–2009) with elaboration of the design in partnership with Viktors Valgums (1948) and Normunds Pavārs (1944). Viktors Valgums was the author of a spatial concept. When working

1. Riga, Brīvības bulvāris (Freedom Boulevard), 1998. (Photo: Rolf Reiner Maria Borchard.)
2. Ernests Pole, former Riga Tradesmen's Savings and Loan, Krišjāņa Barona iela 14, Riga, 1910. Since 1957 used by the National Library. (Photo: National Library of Latvia.)

on the image of the Library, the architects focused on a skyline composition of the Pārdaugava area and on functional aspects of the building. A technological scheme of the Library consisted of a book depository rising 40 metres high and of reading rooms arranged on four levels in the wing facing the River Daugava.

The USSR used this design for the Library building to spruce up its image. In Paris, in the autumn of 1977, at the exhibition at the Centre Pompidou, an elegant wooden model of the Library building was presented and its architecture was highly acclaimed and appreciated by UNESCO. Unfortunately, the model was not returned to Riga and the news of its success did not spread to Latvia. All the attempts of the leaders of the Latvian SSR to make the construction of the Library part of the USSR State Plan for Construction failed. The design itself was highly praised by fellow architects and it has earned its place in the history of Latvia's architecture.

In 1983, the building of the State Library at Jauniela 26 in the historic centre of Riga was dispossessed and the Library was again relocated to the premises of the former fish cannery Kaija at Tērbatas (then Stučkas) iela 75. It only shows how low the prestige of the State Library had been and how unwilling were the authorities to address this matter thoroughly.

At the end of the 1980s, articles about the deplorable state of the Library premises started regularly appearing in the Latvian press. Although there already was the above mentioned design, in 1988 the government of the Latvian SSR decided to hold a competition for the best proposal for construction of the building of the Library of the Latvian SSR named after Vilis Lācis in Riga. The Awakening Movement gathered momentum and it was clear that the collapsing Soviet regime had no funds for construction of cultural buildings. The competition was a complete failure, namely, only four competition entries were submitted.

At that time state officials failed to give a clear answer why the design, which was elaborated back in 1977, was not implemented. I remember quite well how the competition that was a disaster was discussed at the House of Architects at the Swedish Gate and how the idea to approach Gunnar Birkerts caught on. In 1988 it was a revolutionary idea in terms of organisational, financial and ideological aspects. But Gunārs Asaris, the chief architect of Riga, was quick to act and at Christmas in 1988 he phoned Gunnar Birkerts with a request to elaborate a design for the National Library of Latvia (then it was still the Library of the Latvian SSR named after Vilis Lācis). Birkerts replied that it would be a great honour and responsibility for him. One of the most renowned Latvian architects Modris Ģelzis who was also the author of the aforementioned design for the Library building created in 1977 was chosen to work as Birkerts' partner in Latvia.

Since 1989, Andris Vilks, director of the National Library, has been in charge of developing the project concept – now already for 25 years. The idea of a new building of the National Library has been his mission, responsibility and life's work.

In 1989, Gunnar Birkerts made the first sketch, and at this stage of design development it was the architect's present to his homeland. The unusual shape of the building surprised everyone in Latvia and at the same time it evoked positive emotions. A metaphor, a reference to the great Latvian poet Rainis, to Latvia's scenery and folklore – such an interpretation was a complete novelty.

In 1989, the attached title »Library of the Latvian SSR named after Vilis Lācis« was finally removed and it again became the State Library of Latvia. In 1991, the Latvian government decided that from then on the State Library of Latvia would bear the name of the National Library of Latvia and would be part of the international network of national libraries. In 1990, the design of the National Library was presented at the First Baltic-Nordic Architecture Triennial in Tallinn.

In 1995, the first sketch of the design was completed intending to construct the building with the total area of 77,000 square metres. The same year it was decided to significantly reduce its size. Between 1996 and 2000, the second version of the design was developed aiming for the total area of 45,000 square metres. The process had been dragging on and the impatient public started expressing doubts about the necessity of the National Library building. To reinforce the idea of the National Library, in 1989 the Latvian National Library Foundation was established, the intellectual elite of Latvia's society started actively supporting construction of the Library, while the views of different politicians greatly varied. The international acclaim for Birkerts' design echoed also in Latvia and it provided a rare opportunity to use this building – a symbol – to raise awareness of our country. The real international success was »Resolution for the Support to the Construction of the National Library of Latvia« adopted in 1999 by the UNESCO General Assembly. Previously, only once UNESCO had expressed its support for construction of a particular library, i.e. for the Library of Alexandria designed by Norwegian architects (Snohetta). In 2000, a special committee of UNESCO experts was set up to supervise the designing and construction of the National Library of Latvia. The third version of the design, which was completed in 2002, is a result of cooperation between the authors of the design and the UNESCO experts. In 2002, Latvia for the first time participated in the Venice Biennale of Architecture being represented by Gunnar Birkerts's design for the National Library. That year the Bank of Latvia issued a commemorative coin dedicated to the National Library of Latvia.

In 2004, gradual clearance of the site began, houses were removed and their residents compensated, and at the end of 2005, an agreement was reached with Hill International, an international construction consulting firm, on development of the technical design and supervision of construction works. On 20 June 2008, as a result of a joint effort of many people who had kept the faith and worked hard for 20 years, the construction of the National Library building began. In 2009 and 2010 Latvia was seriously affected by the global financial crisis, and construction works were completed only on 20 December 2013.

The opening ceremony marking Riga's becoming the European Capital of Culture 2014 was an emotional and unifying moment for the nation when on 18 January book lovers created a 2014-metre long human chain to transfer the first books from hand to hand from the old premises to the new library building that is proudly called the Castle of Light. The official opening ceremony of the National Library of Latvia was held on the 95th anniversary of the Library on 29 August 2014.

Cityscape

Analysing the National Library within the urban context, it should be emphasized that the site where the Library stands today was chosen neither by organisers of previous competitions nor the author. Its location on the left riverbank of the Daugava (formerly Klīversala embankment) was determined already in 1968 and marked in the Spatial Development Strategy for Riga. The site possessed such spatial qualities as the edifice with elaborate façades and accentuated corner designed by outstanding Latvian architect Eižens Laube, the house designed in an eclectic manner at Uzvaras bulvāris 2 and also a school building designed by Reinhold Schmaeling, former City Architect of Riga, standing slightly farther away on the corner of Uzvaras bulvāris and Raņka dambis. Could the building of the National Library have been contextual in the traditional meaning of this term? It seems not. The original version of the design with its extended programme established a dialogue with the urban environment through the massing where spaces of reading rooms and administrative offices were jutting out thus visually creating a building of two different scales. After the reduction of the planned size in 1995, the other variant, by contrast, abandoned the idea of placing the building over Akmeņu iela and arranging its entrance towards the River Daugava in the centre of the linear structure. The laconic sculptural shape of the completed building is a free-standing structure whose footprint respects the principles of perimetre construction in the site plan, while its entrance facing Uzvaras bulvāris and Akmens Bridge makes it appear more dynamic and establishes good links with the main pedestrian and public transport flows.

Spatially, the building of the National Library is part of the urban ensemble on the left riverbank of the Daugava which consists of a high-rise area where a bank building soaring 121 metres high and round twin towers designed by architect Helmut Jahn stand out among others, of clusters of wooden houses in Ķīpsala which form a low-rise built-up area, the office building of the *Diena* newspaper and the Riga Plaza shopping centre with its ambitious scale and large façades sporting the blue-black-white tricolour of the Estonian flag. If the built-up area in the southern end of Ķīpsala clearly forms a vertical accent, then the new building of the National Library stands out with its idiosyncrasy. It may claim to be a symbol and an urban landmark of Riga and this claim is based on its function and location directly opposite Old Riga.

The concept and the spatial context

Dividing the city into two parts, the River Daugava is undoubtedly the main axis of Riga's spatial composition. The new building of the Library is a herald of a new direction of development of the city centre, and while being located close to the historic centre of Riga that is inscribed on the World Heritage List, it is still separated from this territory where new architecture is bound by the context and strict restrictions to the scale by a stretch of water running half a kilometre wide. Thus, the building of the National Library is in a privileged situation spatially and lawfully thanks to its excellent location and relative freedom of spatial expression. Like the British, who refer to the continental part of Europe as overseas, inhabitants of Riga also call the district on the other side of the river the area across the Daugava – across the water, across the bridge, namely, Pārdaugava. In this regard, it is interesting how Gunnar Birkerts in 2002 described his approach to architecture in the interview with Kay Kaiser, the American architecture critic and author of the book and many articles about Birkerts:

»Architecture is like a very long bridge. One end is anchored on a very solid bearing point that is rooted deep in history. The other end is not anchored at all, but is reaching toward in the future.

I can distinguish the differences in the footsteps on the bridge. There are the heavy, significant strides of the true masters. Some are dogmatically marching in the frozen cadence of their architecture. Coming up behind them are the fast steps of those who are running in fear of growing old. Their fear makes them accept every fashion that comes along and betray the solid foundation laid by those who walked before them. As the old ones approach the end of this imaginary bridge, a new group of masters are just beginning to cross. They do not care about being fashionable. They are non-dogmatic, versatile, flexible, elastic and very competent. They will find the appropriate solution to the problems and their signatures will not be printed heavily over their architecture. A discriminating eye, however, will know it as theirs. This is the group I hope I am in.«

This building is Birkerts' homecoming project, and as he returns to Latvia from the USA, crossing the broad expanse of the ocean, the readers cross the bridge from Old Riga to access the new Library building. When developing the architectural concept of the building, Birkerts used space freely, and it was entirely his idea to use allusions to folklore and symbols characteristic of the Latvian National Awakening and restored independence. The perception of the National Library from three bridges moving across the River Daugava and from the promenades along the embankment determines its spatial qualities and significance. It accounts for a distinctively unique silhouette of the building, its symbolism and literary renditions. The silhouette of the National Library consolidates space around itself and with its pyramidal structure rising 68 metres high it dominates the skyline and even counterbalances the high-rises of Riga's new financial and business district located a few hundred metres northwards.

It is the pyramidal structure that allows the building to create a dialogue with Old Riga's skyline across the river running half a kilometre wide, and at the same time effortlessly taking over the vacant territory between the building and the embankment. Originally Birkerts had intended to build a wide pedestrian platform over the street and ensure free access to the embankment; however, the completed street crossing is much simpler. Landscape and improvement elements form an unpretentious base of the Library building with the planes of lawns rising upwards from the Daugava and surrounding streets. The ramp providing access to the service area on the south side of the building and a small amphitheatre opening towards the Daugava blend naturally within the terrain. The arrangement of pedestrian paths in the large area extending towards the street and the embankment, which resembles a

3. Illustration to Jānis Rainis, *Zelta Zirgs* (The Golden Horse), 1909.
4. Gunnar Birkerts, National Library of Latvia, concept sketch.

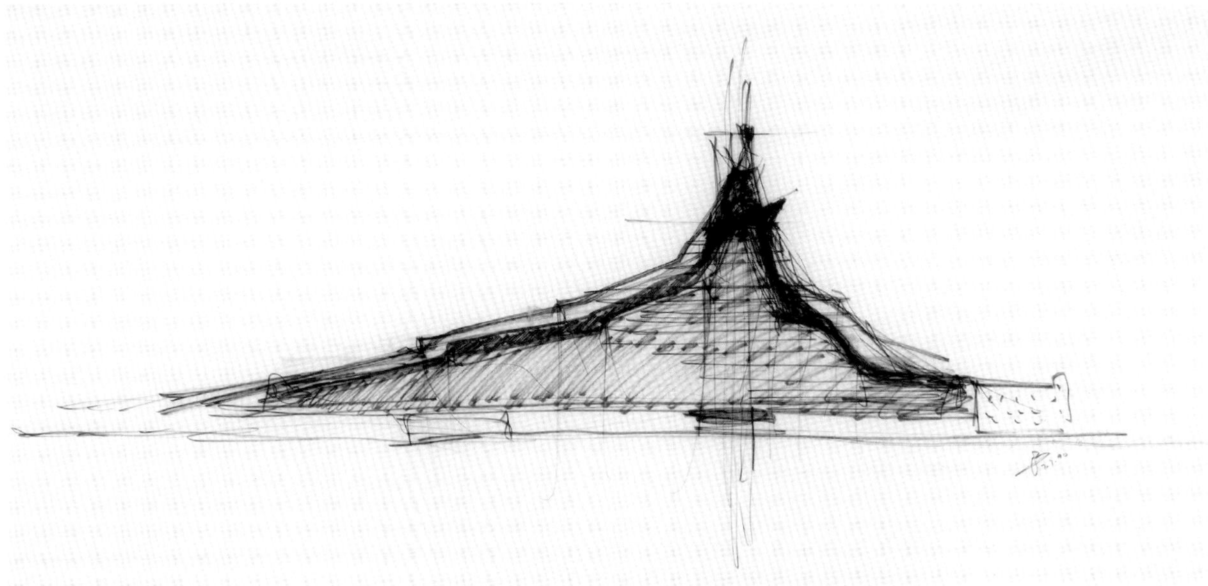

geometric tangle of roots, establishes functional links and harmoniously relates to the architectural idiom of the building. The use of granite slabs and paving in a large belt along the façade facing the Daugava makes the surrounding area aesthetically appealing and sustainable and also sets a scene for various public events and adds an outdoor space to the Library's restaurant. The geometric pattern becomes even more dynamic in the entrance area where granite slabs of contrasting shades have been used. Thus, it correlates directly with the way how the entrance grows diagonally into the linear structure of the building and into its functional and simple layout.

Massing of the building

It took such a long time to build the National Library that it has become a subject of the legend. At various points in time, we, in Latvia, have called the library building »a gigantic ship of books«, referring to its location on the riverbank of the Daugava, »a crystal palace« due to the frailty of its glass walls, »the great bookcase« and a »time capsule« referring to its capacity for storage of eight million copies of printed materials. It has also been called »the mountain of glass«, alluding to the insurmountable mountain of glass in the symbol-laden play written by Jānis Rainis, the most famous Latvian poet, and »the castle of light«, emphasising the importance of its content and the opportunity to research and learn that it represents. Despite endless discussions about the building and its shape, over the entire 25-year period Birkerts never changed the concept of its massing. Neither did he change his modernist conviction in his 65-year-long career in architecture. The original motif of the mountain of glass borrowed from Rainis' play persisted, and, as project development continued, it naturally evolved into the concept of »The Castle of Light« – and they both stem from content and form. It is, indeed, rare for so many narrative elements to be tastefully amalgamated into architecture. And this is one of those rare cases that has also been highly acclaimed internationally since leading Italian, German, British and American journals of architecture had published articles about the library project even before the beginning of construction works. This resulted in extensive forerunning international publicity and in appreciation and recognition of the Latvian state, its construction sector, culture and ability. Referring to the launch of the book *Gunnar Birkerts: Metaphoric Modernist* in 2009, architecture critic Norman Weinstein published an article in the *AchNewsNow* newsletter and his comments prove that this project was not a mere presumption nurtured by Latvian provincialism. Weinstein concludes that the project of the National Library is destined to promote the little-known culture of Latvia beyond Europe and that its subtle allusions to Latvian folklore will make the building an object of architectural tourism. Weinstein predicts that Birkerts' National Library of Latvia will be as positively provocative as the Seattle Central Library designed by Koolhaas.

However, the attitude of Latvia's society and political elite towards the idea of having a new building of the National Library has been changeable over a period of 25 years – short-term social programmes, national security or teachers' salaries are the issues that always prevail over other concerns in a new country. What was initially a nationwide unifying idea later was severely criticised due to the relatively high construction costs of the building. For two decades Birkerts and advocates of the Library idea had to explain patiently why the new building was necessary and why its image was so significant.

In this context, it is important what Gunnar Birkerts had to say in this regard: »Although it is possible to link one culture with other ones by means of instant electronic information exchange, the main task of the Library is to store and preserve our cultural heritage. The Library's archives store our literature and historical documents, our folklore – our DNA. It is a witness of the destiny of our nation. The image of the building speaks out loud. The Library turns into a functional national symbol.«

Large public buildings are often destined to become symbols of a city or a state. Public buildings also demonstrate power or superior ability. This phenomenon in its hypertrophied form can be seen in Astana, Baku, Dubai and elsewhere in the world, but it also has another dimension that is propelling technological advancement in a reasonable and guiding way while also creating identity.

The building of the National Library of Latvia also combines architecture, symbols, technology, power, ability and identity. And that is why the building provokes so much discussion and dispute. This process shows the society in cross-section where pride and joy intermingle with ambition, political speculation and generosity of donators, and where far-sightedness of the nation coexists alongside narrow-mindedness of consumer society.

As the project kept evolving over time, the massing of the building acquired accentuated expressiveness, since a steady linear inclination of the large structure towards and over the street was replaced by steep verticality of stainless steel planes. Traditional elements fitted to the urban scale that were protruding from the façades in the original version have blended into a single structure with dynamic vertical bands of window openings. The southern façade at a close-up and from a distance appears sculpturally laconic. Its unique silhouette makes it stand out in the urban environment while the protruding horizontal lines of suspended stainless steel sun protectors covering the area of 600 square metres make it appear intriguing at a close-up. There are some technically interesting details and an attractive interplay of light. The radically distinctive outline of the façade facing the River Daugava is accentuated in a wider urban area by means of light illumination focusing on the recessed transparent bands running along the façade. The transparent part of the façade includes a specially designed shade ensuring a transition to plastic windows that provide the necessary comfort in reading rooms and in public spaces located on the upper floors. In fact, the expressiveness of the two façades is achieved through the use of four types of high-quality building materials covering the area of 15,617 square metres.

If the overall image of the pyramidal building during the design elaboration has not substantially deviated from the idea of »the castle of light« and »the mountain of glass«, then the massing of the two façades and the applied means of expression have undergone significant changes. However, as regards the content, conceptually the façade towards the Daugava has retained its original source of inspiration. It still includes some direct references to the sketches made in the 1980s-90s. Thus, the façade facing the river displays the verticality characteristic of Latvia's birch groves.

The façade towards Pārdaugava avoids any interpretations relating to the urban fabric as to the transition from a scale of Riga's streetscape to the pyramidal edifice. In the completed building the two façades with two distinct silhouettes in the process of detail elaboration have acquired two distinguishing visual features i.e. strong horizontal arrangement in the southern façade that hides all offices of the National Library, and strong vertical arrangement of the recessed window openings in the wing containing reading rooms.

Structure and materials

The building is a reinforced concrete structure arranged on 13 levels (one underground level) with a metal frame structure on two levels at the top of the building. The building rests on piles the total length of which is 8,900 metres. The façades are made of tinted 4-layer glass panels which together with the windows cover the area of 13,900 square metres. The total area of roof planes is 7,400 square metres. The western and eastern façades are made of stainless steel. The whole structure rests on the foundations made of monolithic concrete and thermal insulation panels that are inserted in water-resistant metal casing. The total weight of steel roof panels is 607 tons.

The choice of building materials determines the nature and visual appearance of the edifice. The idea of the »glass mountain« does not necessary mean that the building is made of glass. The author has always emphasized that the National Library is the building with a particularly important function rendered in solemn tones.

To a large extent, shades and tones of the materials used in the exterior can also be seen in the interior – glass, granite in different shades of grey, silvery-white matte and lustrous metal, wood.

Layout

The linear structure of the building runs parallel to Valguma Street, the total length of the structure is 170 metres, width – 44 metres, and height – 68.3 metres. The layout is simple and functional. A special board of international experts appointed by UNESCO and specialists from the National Library supervised the entire process of its development and alteration. The National Library is divided into five functional areas, where reading rooms take up the largest part or 28 percent, public spaces 23 percent, auxiliary rooms 19 percent, rooms and offices for the staff 18 percent and storage facilities of printed materials 12 percent.

The large auditorium/concert hall with 450 seats, a book shop, exhibition halls with the floor space of 470 square metres, a book museum, a café and a restaurant are arranged at the entrance level, around the central lobby. The auditorium at the entrance level shares the same function with the conference centre located at the underground level and covering the area of 1,450 square metres.

All reading rooms and exhibition halls open towards the Daugava and have amazing views across the river to Old Riga. Rooms and offices of the staff of the National Library and other institutions align the southern façade. The pride and glory of the interior is a spacious atrium in the central part of the building which spatially combines eight levels providing natural daylight to the public spaces. In the central part there are book storages on six levels, the large auditorium and auxiliary rooms. Both level 9 and level 10 are fully provided for technical facilities.

Technical maintenance of the building is planned from the ramp embedded in the relief between the building itself and Valguma Street which provides an easy access to technical facilities at the underground level, as well as to the conference halls and the concert hall/auditorium.

Interior and furniture

Both the author of the design and his Latvian partners have defined their interior concept of the National Library as follows: »The architecture of the interior of The Castle of Light is strict, and even clean – if we can say

5. Gunnar Birkerts, 2008. (Photo: Dainis Bušmanis.)

so. No direct contemporary clichés have been used. Components, materials and their colours were chosen so as to please both visual and tactile senses, as well as to ensure their durability, focusing first and foremost on one thing – how to highlight the centrepiece – *the book.*«

Being a quintessential embodiment of the silver grey colour scheme, the uniting spacious lobby at the entrance level is an area that is accessible to large audiences and that leads to other functions of the Library. The overall impression is made up by stone flooring and glossy and matte metal surfaces used in the finish of walls, ceilings and columns. On the floor polished and cut granite slabs are combined into clear ethnographic patterns that have been used in the Latvian textiles for centuries. Light wooden parts of some wall fragments make the large public space appear cosier.

The impressive atrium is divided into two parts with open stairs linking six levels. The first section of the atrium is overlooked by peculiarly shaped skylights rising above the façade, while an effective bookshelf reaching 21 metres high adorns its second section and the entire Library building as a spatial and thematic accent. Its sloping glass wall greets the visitor and ensures a permanent presence of the book in the public spaces of the Library. The giant bookshelf also reflects the composition of the layout, i.e. it crowns seven levels of storage rooms of books and other printed materials totalling to 6.5 million units.

In interviews, Birkerts has always emphasized that the expressive and distinctly peculiar shape of the building was not an obstacle for furnishing the interior in classically modern Scandinavian style exuding an aura of Nordic austerity. Birkerts has always admired and held Aalto and Asplund's works in high esteem, and his career in architecture began in Saarinen's office. The use of wood as a finish material in interiors is so characteristic of Scandinavian architecture (and also of Birkerts' works and of our contemporary Latvian architecture), and it can also be seen in the interior architecture of the auditorium/concert hall of the National Library where the arrangement of wooden planes of various textures brings out both acoustic and architectural qualities hinting at restrained expressiveness.

The furnishings of the National Library account for the overall aura of the interior: the public area located around the entrance lobby and the atrium visually blends with the reading rooms, since it is merely a glass wall that physically separates these areas. Therefore, the architect's choice of materials, their compatibility, harmony of colours and textures used in the wall finish and flooring, and the design of the furniture acquire a special meaning. Unpretentiousness of various shades of grey of different stone and metal surfaces, carpets and walls (undoubtedly, one of the masterstrokes in the interior design of the National Library) acquires another (background) quality serving as a perfect foil for the prevailing lightness and warmth of natural birch furniture that is pleasant to touch.

If the design of bookshelves is pragmatic and functional, then the perfect balance between the surface and the support of reading tables is a good example of great elegance and durability which alludes to the architecture of the building. References to the expressive vocabulary of modernist architecture are more direct (and this can be clearly seen in Birkerts' sketches for these groups of furniture) in the design of the furniture of information centres in various reading rooms.

Round tables in the information areas of reading rooms and sets of furniture standing out with their bright colours and distinctive shapes that are interspersed between reading rooms and in the public area complement the overall geometric arrangement. This is the zone where colours start to interplay with the system of navigation markers and graphic signs of the building what complies with the architectural concept of the building and document A117.1-1998 of the International Code Council and American National Standards Institute (ANSI). The entire system consists of 17 groups of signs, namely, functional markers, floor plans with a traditional red dot – *you are here*, 16 pictograms with different meanings, stationary and portable information stands or captions under works of art displayed in the building. All pictograms fit into square-shaped spaces of various sizes, and their symbols are white on the background reproduced in 14 different hues relating to the colours used on the Latvian national currency the lat that was replaced by the euro in 2014. The typeface Avenir in light, medium and heavy weights has been used for all signs, markers and captions. In addition to the mentioned 17 groups of signs, there are two that are particularly important, namely, the letters making up the name »Latvijas Nationālā Bibliotēka« (National Library of Latvia) to the right of the entrance and the Wall of Supporters in the entrance lobby (a simple stainless steel frame that graphically depicts donations of various amounts). The name of the building blends harmoniously with the architecture of the building, the design of the public transport stop, and in particular, with the slanting roof of the building.

From a sketch to the design of the letters at the entrance of the Library and to 648 rooms with different functions and to a glass crown at the top, it took 25 long years and a lot of patience to complete this building that is Birkerts' masterpiece.

Why Birkerts?

In the context of the National Library of Latvia both aspects are interesting and important, namely, the overall image of Gunnar Birkerts' architecture as a key to understanding the spatial idiom of the Library building, and professional, political and emotional attributes characterizing Birkerts as the author of the building.

It was a daring act of civil liberty and thinking outside the box imposed by the system when at Christmas, in 1988, three years before the collapse of the Soviet regime, Gunārs Asaris, chief architect of Riga, called Gunnar Birkerts and suggested that he designed the National Library of Latvia. However, there were at least four preconditions prompting such a deed, i.e. Birkerts is of Latvian descent and his family had played a special role in the cultural history of Latvia; Birkerts had personally visited Latvia several times in the 1980s and given public lectures on architecture; Birkerts' extensive experience in designing of libraries and eight outstanding library projects completed by that time in the USA; and the unsuccessful design competition for the new building of the National Library in 1988.

»I was born, more or less, under the same constellation as modern architecture, and very near to the birthday of Bauhaus«, Birkerts says. And it is true, he was born on 17 January 1925 and his childhood years coincided with Latvia's first and brief period of independence between the two world wars. His parents Pēteris Birkerts (1881–1956) and Merija Shop Birkerts (1894–1982) came from the academically educated intelligentsia of Latvia who had started to research and classify treasures of Latvian cultural heritage, especially folklore, even before 1918, when the State of Latvia was founded. Birkerts' father Pēteris, a renowned creativity psychologist, writer, folklorist and philosopher, was one of the most highly educated people in Latvia of his time. Birkerts' mother was a linguist, folklorist and teacher who was loved by her students. The conceptually dense spiritual heritage and influence of his parents on the future architect allows Kay Kaiser, an architecture critic and researcher of Birkerts' work, to conclude: »Latvia's symbols, mythology and literature shaped him before he could walk down the streets on his own. Indigenous and ancient folk songs, parables, riddles and sayings expressed the national spirit. Birkerts inherited their (parents) verbal ability. The symbols, wit and accessible metaphors that are in his architecture came from this exposure. Birkerts' interest in the psychological implications of design can be traced to his father.«[1]

We often speak about the soul and musicality of buildings. I believe it should be emphasised also speaking about Birkerts as an architect – in his youth he used to sing in a choir (Latvians are, indeed, a real choral singing nation!), play the violin and the piano. Remarkably, the piano of the Birkerts family (the same that the master of architecture played in his childhood) now stands and is played in the public area on the top floor of the Library building.

Along with the influence of his parents and their social activities, Riga as a Nordic metropolis and a Hanseatic city with its distinctive spatial composition and the proximity of the Baltic Sea have also shaped Birkerts' interests and the early development of his personality.

In 1938, Birkerts started seriously studying sciences as well as the German and English languages at Riga Gymnasium No 1. While still a schoolboy, at the age of 13, Birkerts decided to become an architect: it was a spontaneous decision made after seeing an architectural sketch drawn by an older schoolmate and displayed at an exhibition dedicated to the choice of future profession. In 1941, the Birkerts family experienced the first Soviet occupation and, in 1944, at the end of WWII when the second Soviet occupation was imminent, Gunnar Birkerts together with the family of his friend Augusts Grasis left for Germany and settled in Nördlingen. When the war ended in 1945 Birkerts withstood a competition from other foreign students and was accepted at the Technische Hochschule in Stuttgart. He left Nördlingen with his best friend Grasis, who became his roommate in Stuttgart and later an engineer and industrialist based in Kansas City. All his life Augusts Grasis remained Birkerts' best friend whom the master has also designed two private houses.

At the age of 20 when he began studying at the university, Birkerts understood that it was his big chance. »Now I had the end of the rope, and from now I had to do the pulling. According to my strengths, I would either make it or not«, he says. If German students wanted to dedicate their knowledge and work to the recovery of the country after the devastating war or were immersed in an interesting theoretical dispute between the Bauhaus and Heimatstil directions in architecture, then Birkerts focused on the global developments in architecture, especially in the USA and Scandinavia where such great masters of architecture as Alvar Aalto, Eliel and Eero Saarinen, Erik Gunnar Asplund, Sven Markelius practised. Even then, Birkerts concluded that only dogma was to follow the dogma. Professor Rolf Gutbrod with his independent way of thinking, a synthesized approach to the analysis of architectural processes and his life style was a great source of influence on young Birkerts during his university years. In their conversations the professor introduced Birkerts to the architectural principles used by Hans Scharoun and Rudolf Steiner.

At the end of 1949, Birkerts graduated from the university in Stuttgart having obtained thorough and practical knowledge of the old world and a diploma of an architect and engineer issued by the Technical University. However, Birkerts was eager to see the new world and on 17 December 1949, one month before his twenty-fifth birthday, his ship arrived in New York harbour after an eleven-day passage from Bremerhaven.

Unlike the previous part of Birkerts' biography that was defined mostly by his parents, history and WWII, the years Birkerts spent in the USA were shaped by his own intellect, talent and professional diplomacy. However, two facts should be mentioned. Firstly, his father Pēteris Birkerts had already trodden a path to America for his son when he arrived in the USA in 1905 and studied law at Valparaiso University in Indiana and, after graduation, studied psychology and sociology at New York City's Columbia University. Gunnar Birkerts attempted to enter the University of Michigan as early as in 1947, when he was still studying in Stuttgart. He was not accepted on the grounds that he was not prepared well enough. A mere twelve years passed, and at the kind invitation of the very same university Birkerts started to work as a professor of architecture there. Moreover, he received recognition and honorary titles for his work in professor's capacity from the University of Michigan and from a number of other schools of architecture. Is this sheer chance, coincidence, or destiny?

Secondly, at the very beginning of 1950, Birkerts took the iconic Greyhound bus and, armed with a recommendation letter from Professor Gutbrod, went to Bloomfield Hills, Michigan, to meet Eero Saarinen. However, Saarinen could not offer a job to Birkerts at that time because the project of the General Motors Technical Centre had come to a standstill. Instead, at Eero Saarinen's recommendation, Birkerts worked for a Chicago architecture firm Perkins and Will for a year, then again returned to Saarinen, a renowned master of Scandinavian architecture, under the guidance of which he worked till 1955. Birkerts highly values this period and the following years from 1955 till 1959, when he worked with Minoru Yamasaki, as a period of self-development under the guidance of great contemporary architects of different mentalities. »I had listened long enough. My apprenticeship was over. Now it was my turn to speak«, Birkerts says.

What follows is a success story spanning half a century long and comprising iconic buildings in the USA,

6. Rudolf Steiner, Second Goethenaum, Dornach, 1924–28. (Photo: Thomas Dix.)
7. Hans Scharoun, Berliner Philharmonie, Berlin, 1956 to 1963. (Photo: Reinhard Friedrich.)
8. Eero Saarinen, Kresge Auditorium, Massachusetts Institute of Technology, Cambridge, Mass., 1953–56. (Photo: https://sfclockworkorange.wordpress.com.)
9. Eero Saarinen, MIT Chapel, Massachusetts Institute of Technology, Cambridge, Mass., 1953–56. (Photo: Madcoverboy.)

a number of monographs, theoretical accounts of the creative process, countless photos on the covers of architecture journals, professor's work at the University of Michigan and guest lectures at many schools of architecture all over the world.

Birkerts is a convinced second-generation modernist in a broader sense of this notion, his architecture is organic and contextual in its deepest essence. He works with structures above the ground and underground – he makes light a non-material building material. Birkerts is the architect of light. Birkerts' best works are characterized by the presence of »Zeitgeist« as well as symbols and metaphors. And finally, the expressiveness of his buildings allows Birkerts to be called an expressive modernist what adds an idiosyncratic style to his architecture.

Birkerts himself, critics and his world-renowned colleagues have come up with conclusive statements about the architect's creative method and individual buildings. The quotations given below provide a more comprehensive insight on the building of the National Library of Latvia as seen by Birkerts himself and in the context of Latvian and international architecture.

»If you have a building that has a need, a particular charge to do something; if there is soul somewhere in the programme, that the building has to talk, inspire or project; then this is the biggest challenge: to express the soul, the feeling, the meaning, the essence of what it is and what it does«, said Birkerts referring to the mission of the building and its added value (1983, School of Architecture, University of Illinois) exactly 30 years before the completion of the National Library project. And these are the principles that the Library project embodies.

»He (Birkerts) is indeed a complete architect, very aware of his responsibilities and of the social role that his buildings play. He maintains an unflagging concern for the comfort and pleasure of the users, and for the key relationship among the whole, the parts, and the human scale«, says architect Cesar Pelli.[2]

»His own way« chosen by the architect and some special (iconic) buildings have earned him a place in the global architecture and recognition among fellow architects. Thus, speaking about the author of the National Library of Latvia, we should mention a fusion of conciseness and functionality in the Contemporary Art Museum (Houston, 1970–72), transformation of engineering structures of the building into a striking visual image of the Federal Reserve Bank (Minneapolis, 1967–73), a very successful use of the underground space aimed at preservation of qualities of the historic architecture in the addition to the Law School, University of Michigan (Ann Arbor, 1974–81) and a challenging approach to plasticity of geometric shapes in the Corning Museum of Glass (Corning, NY, 1976–80).

Birkerts has also designed several noteworthy library buildings, namely, Duluth Public Library (Minnesota, 1969–79), Uris Library addition, Cornell University (Ithaca, NY, 1980–83), Central Library expansion, University of California (San Diego, 1987–93) and Dr. Martin Luther King Jr. Library (San Jose, 1998–2004), which combining the needs of the city of San Jose and the San Jose State University covers the same area as the National Library of Latvia.

And the third group of Birkerts' works is characterized by the expressive vocabulary of shapes, the message or the dynamism (expression) present in the building of the National Library of Latvia as well. The papal altar and furniture, Pontiac Silverdome (Pontiac, 1987), of course, is not a building, but the dynamics of broken lines and references to the Pope's message, the analysis of the ritual and behaviour makes this group of objects designed for the Pope's visit stand apart as the work of art in its own right. The peculiar massing of the building of the United States Embassy Office in Venezuela (Caracas, 1989–96) accentuated by horizontal lines running along the façade as well as the overhang at the entrance and the structure of access roads have given expression and articulation to the building restrained by protocol. Kemper Museum of Contemporary Art and Design (Kansas City, 1991 to 1994) demonstrates the diversity of the cultural space through the massing while the façade and the roof (like in the building of the National Library of Latvia) innately form a single composition. The mansion (Vail, Colorado, 1990–94) designed by Birkerts for his best friend Augusts Grasims displays the same qualities. I believe that the addition to the Law School, Ohio State University (Columbus, 1988–93) should also be on this list. The stairs attached to the wing containing offices gives the whole complex, where the library is an essential part,a new direction, dynamics and expression.

Birkerts has always designed with a long-term perspective in mind and has avoided throwing somersaults in an attempt to chase the latest fashion. He also describes the National Library of Latvia as a classical and modern building due to its serious museum-function since the entire collection of the materials printed in Latvia is stored there. The Library building is a long-lasting phenomenon in the building art of the nation. »Architecture is not living in the historical illusions, nor in the utopian projections. Architecture is today being conceived by the minds of today, being built by the hands of today and technology of today. Technology does not prevent one from working with the moods that architecture may have to express, whether they are symbolic or metaphoric. The important thing is to build, to synthesize the needs, the aspirations, the directions in art and life style, to conceive the answers that are buildable, useable. An extension of the past …«[3]

A brief look at the history of the Birkerts' family and master's creative biography, at the buildings he has created and his thoughts about architecture, in my opinion, is a strong argument for the choice of the author of the National Library of Latvia – it is this rare win-win situation which gives Latvia international recognition and a landmark building while its author has a chance to return home with a symbolic building and a crowning achievement of his creative career.

[1] *The Architecture of Gunnar Birkerts,* text by Kay Kaiser, Washington, D.C.,1989.
[2] University of Illinois, School of Architecture, Plym Distinguished Professorship in Architecture, 1983.
[3] From an interview with Charles Gandee, editor, in *Architectural Record*, 1983.

This essay is a continuation of the descriptions and analyses the author has presented in his articles about the National Library of Latvia in the magazine *Latvijas architektūra* (Latvian Architecture) between 2011 and 2014.

1. Gunnar Birkerts, Schwartz Summer Residence, Northville, Michigan, 1960. (Photo: Balthazar Korab.)
2. Gunnar Birkerts, University Reformed Church, Ann Arbor, Michigan, 1963/64). (Photo: Balthazar Korab.)
3. Gunnar Birkerts, Travis Residence, Franklin, Michigan, 1964/65. (Photo: Keiichi Miayshita.)
4. Gunnar Birkerts, Federal Reserve Bank, Minneapolis, Minnesota, 1967–73. (Photo: Balthazar Korab.)
5. Gunnar Birkerts, Duluth Public Library, Duluth, Minnesota, 1969–79. (Photo: Balthazar Korab.)
6. Gunnar Birkerts, Contemporary Arts Museum Houston, Houston, Texas, 1970–72. (Photo: Balthazar Korab.)
7. Gunnar Birkerts, Calvary Baptist Church, Detroit, Michigan, 1974–77. (Photo: Timothy Hursley.)
8. Gunnar Birkerts, The Corning Museum of Glass, Corning, New York, 1976–80. (Photo: Timothy Hursley.)
9. Gunnar Birkerts, Holtzman & Silverman office building, Southfield, Michigan, 1983–89. (Photo: Balthazar Korab.)
10. Gunnar Birkerts, library addition, University of California, San Diego, California, 1987–93. (Photo: Glen Cormier.)
11. Gunnar Birkerts, Church of the Servant, Kentwood, Michigan, 1988–94. (Photo: Timothy Hursley.)
12. Gunnar Birkerts, papal altar and furniture, Pontiac, Michigan, 1987. (Photo: Balthazar Korab.)
13. Gunnar Birkerts, United States Embassy office building, Caracas, Venezuela, 1989–96. (Photo: Gunnar Birkerts.)
14. Gunnar Birkerts, Kemper Museum of Contemporary Art and Design, Kansas City, Missouri, 1991–94. (Photo: Timothy Hursley.)
15. Gunnar Birkerts with Carrier Johnson, Dr. Martin Luther King Jr. Library, San Jose, California, 1998–2004. (Photo: Timothy Hursley.)

1. Aerial view with Riga's historic area on the right, the River Daugava in the centre and the new National Library as an accent of the new development of Riga's city centre.
2. Site plan including the Daugava riverbank.

pp. 18, 19
3. Floor plan of the entrance level including the main auditorium/concert hall, the exhibition area and the restaurant.
4. Floor plan of level –1 including the conference centre and technical rooms.
5. Floor plan of the mezzanine level including the library's information centre, reading rooms and offices.
6. Floor plan of level 2 including reading rooms, book storage and offices.

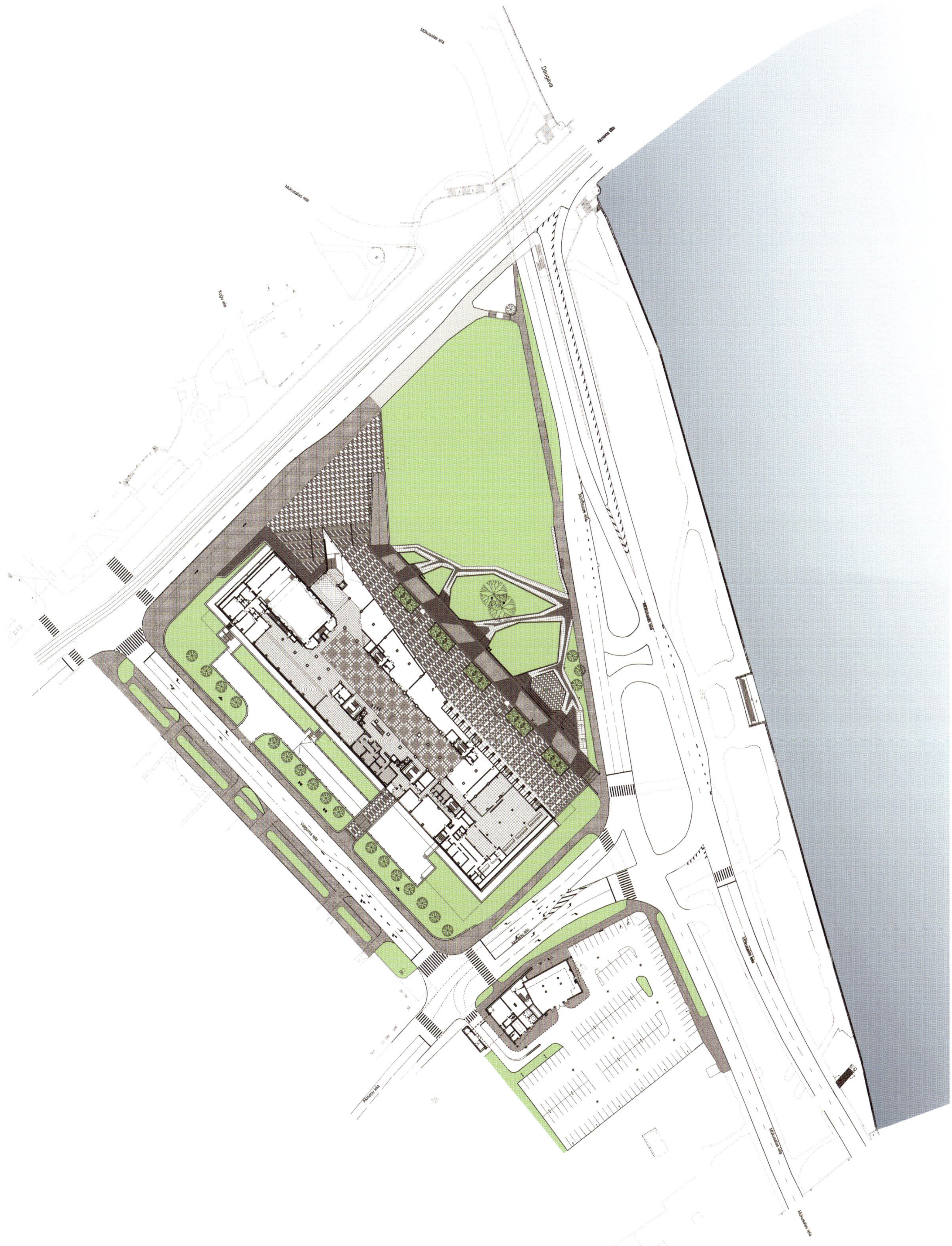

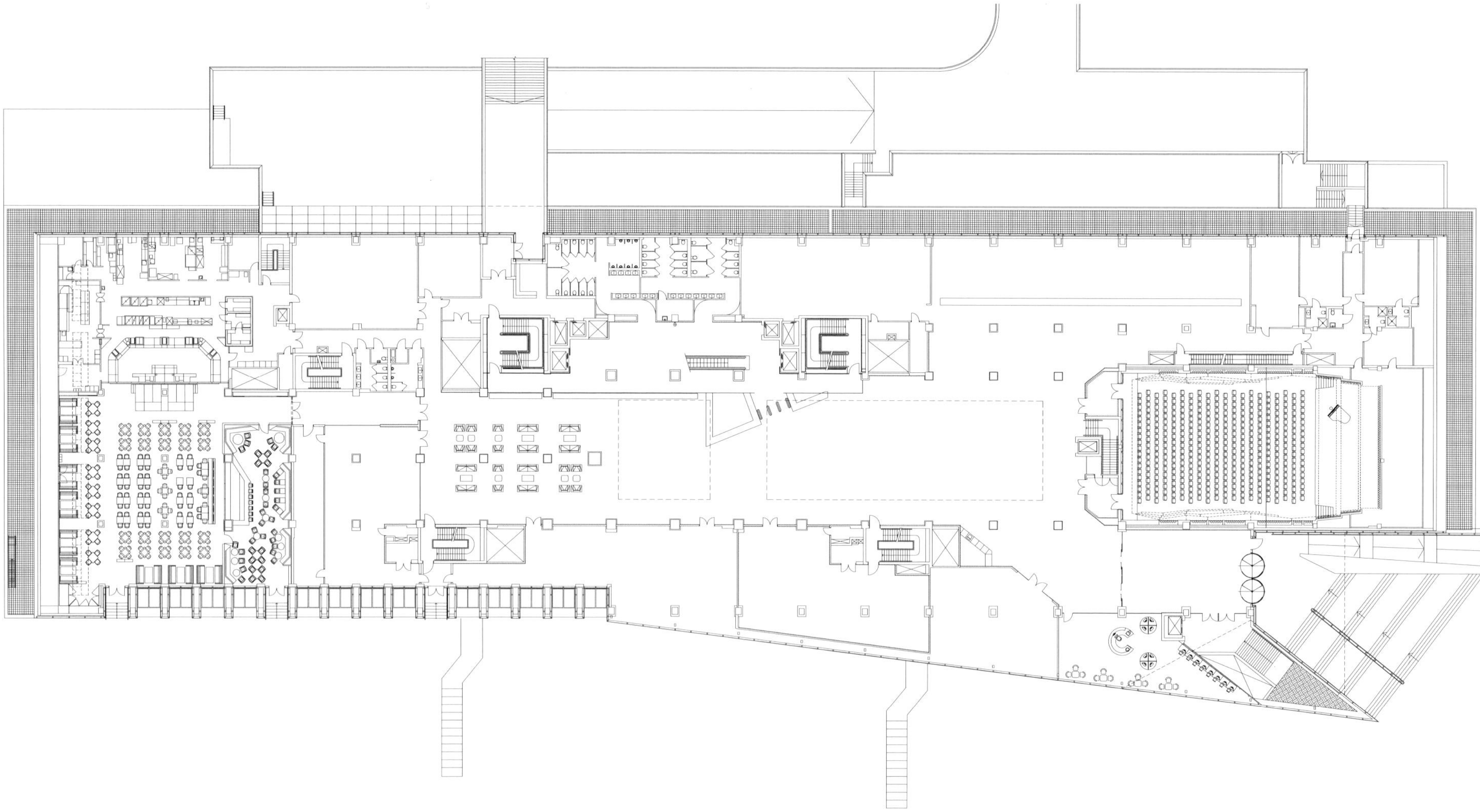

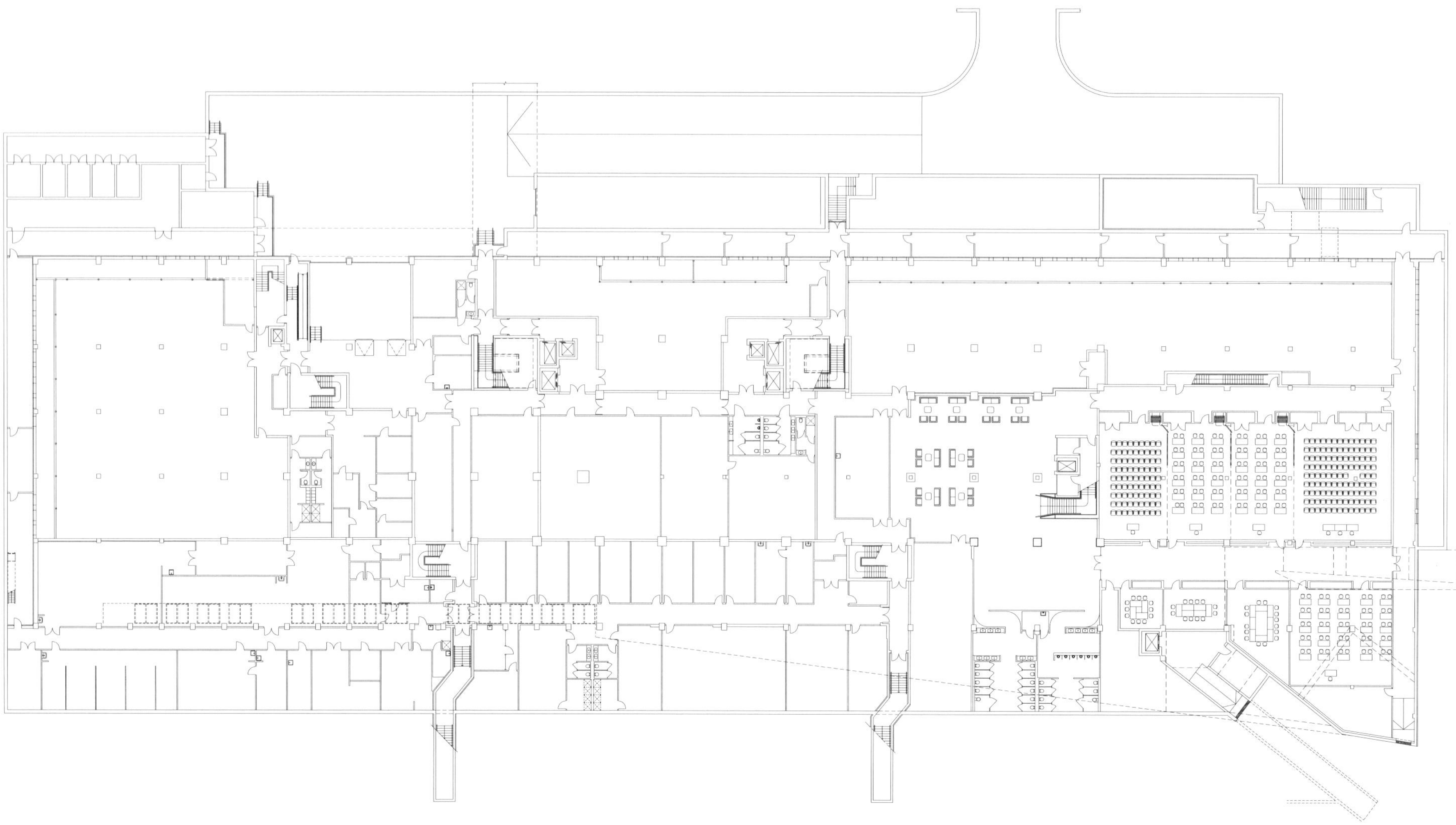

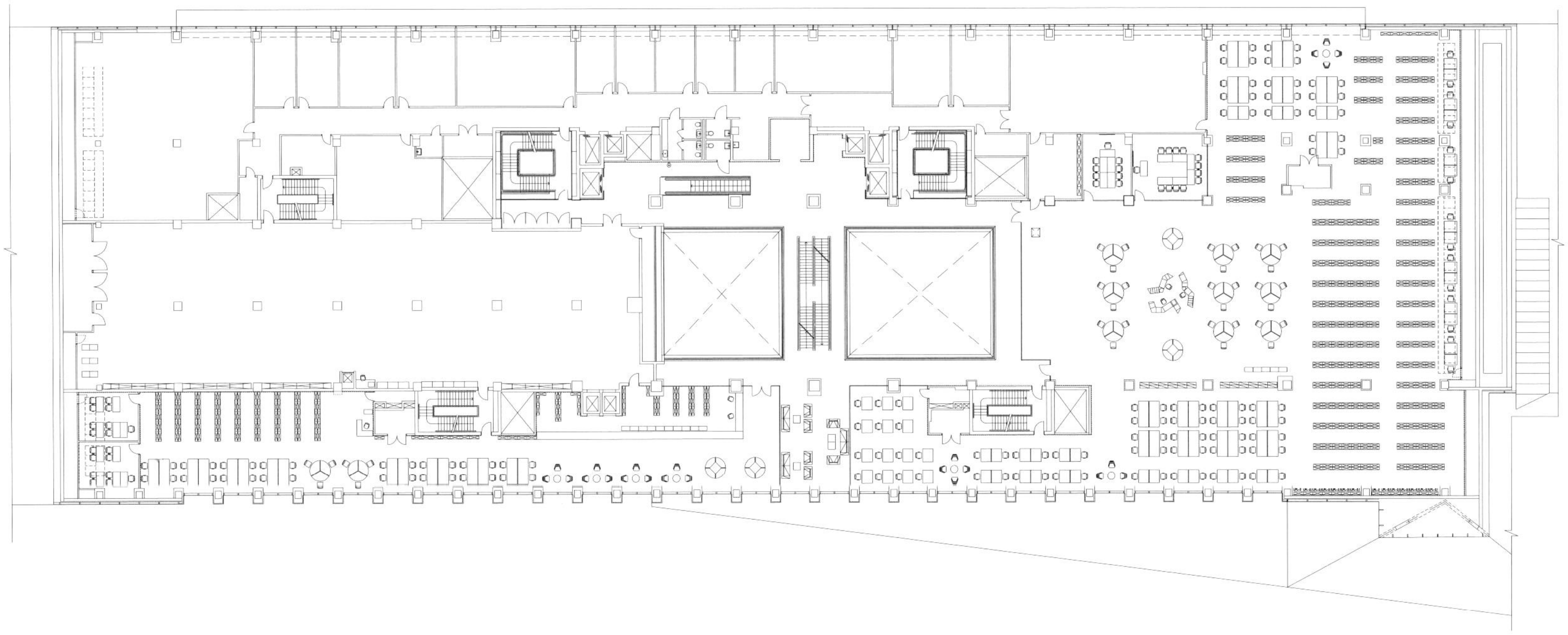

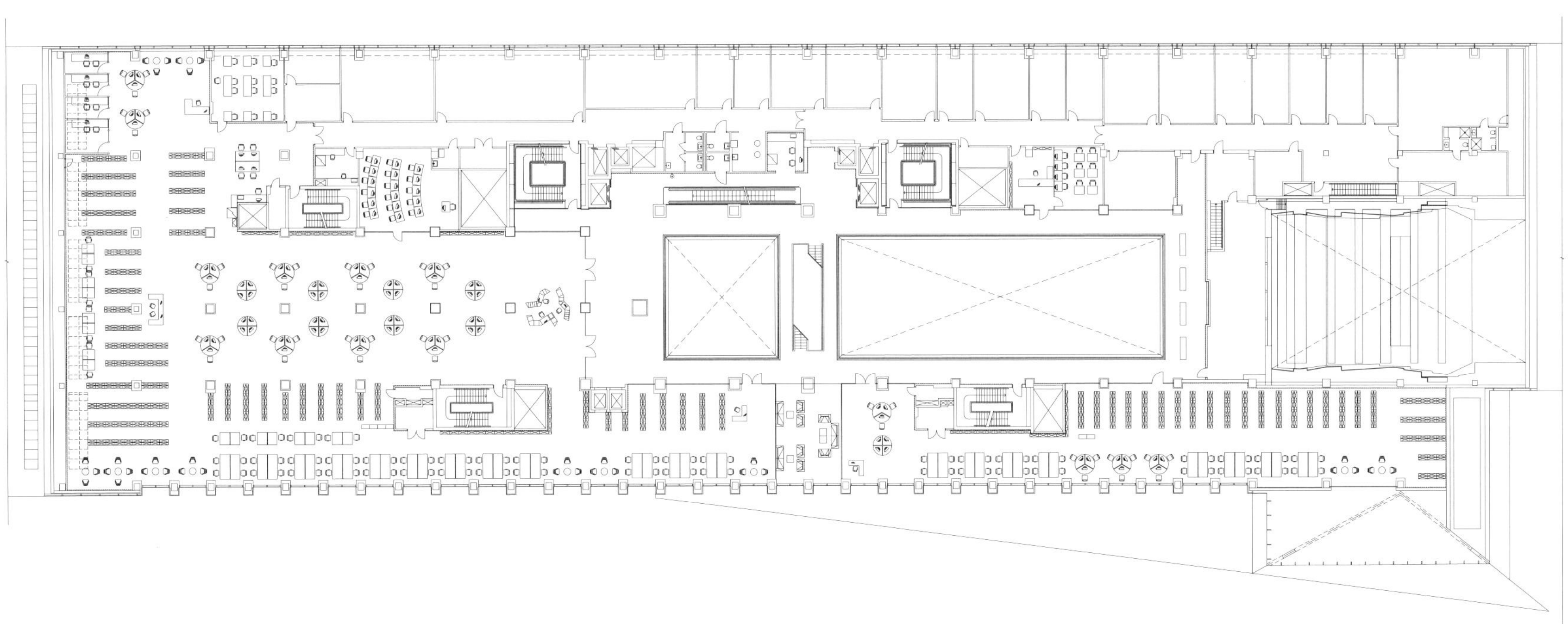

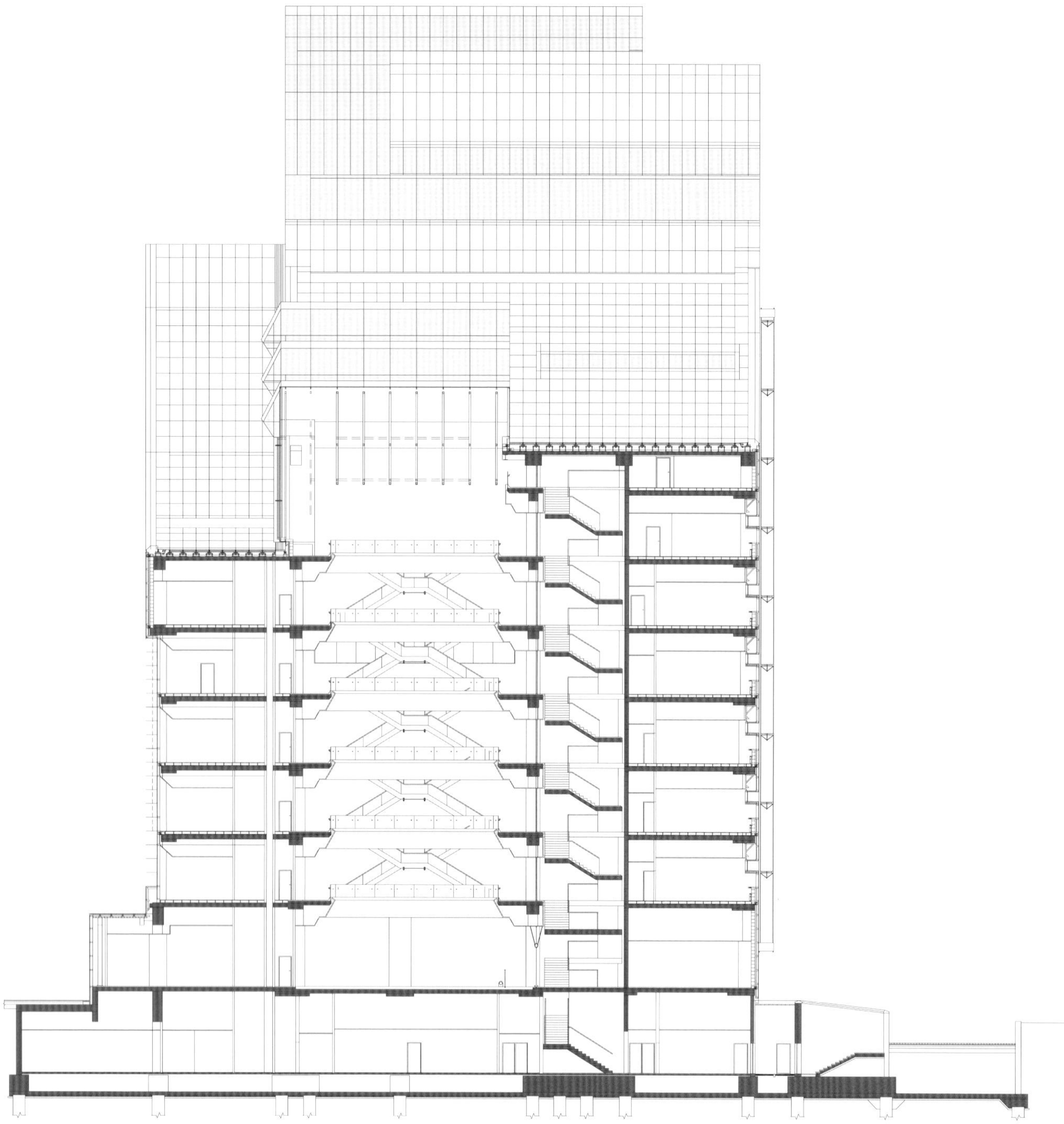

7. Cross section
8. Longitudinal section of the building through the atrium.
9. Section of top levels 11 and 12.

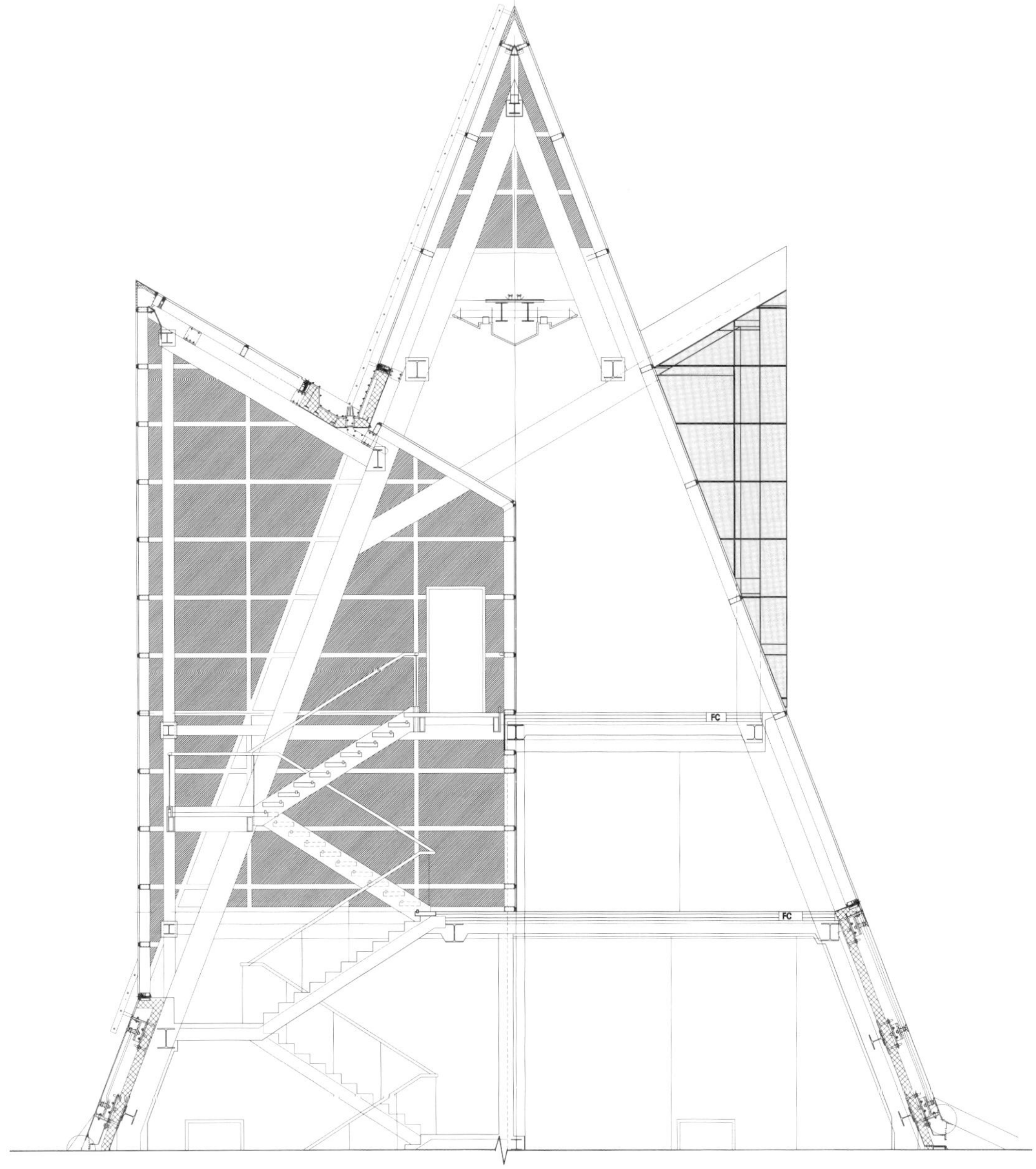

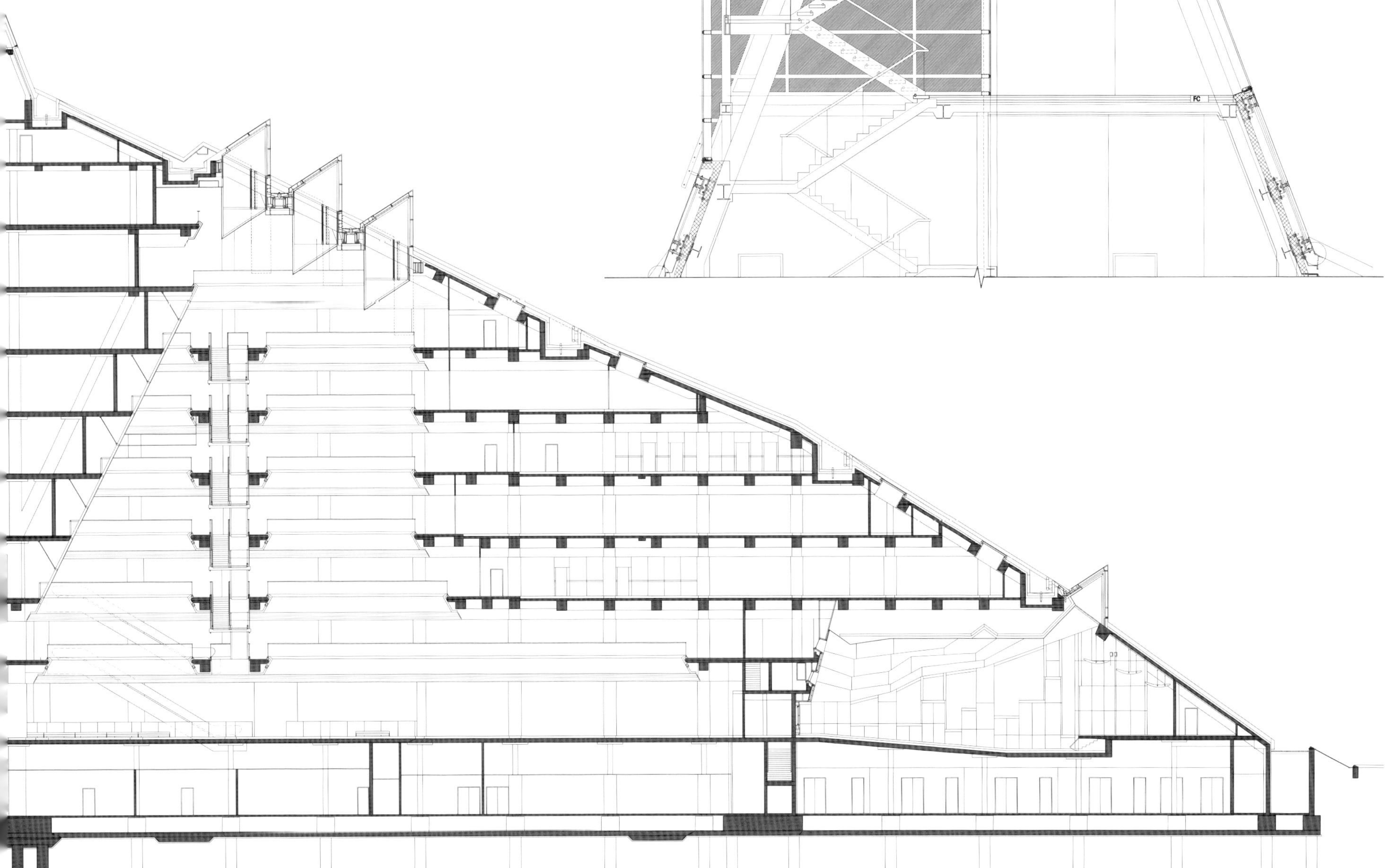

1. Aerial view from the east from the top of the Academy of Sciences.
2. View from the north from the suspension bridge across the River Daugava.

3. View from the north with the main entrance in the foreground.
4. View from the north-west showing the sculpturally laconic south-west façade with the rhythmical lines of stainless steel sun protectors.

pp. 26, 27
5. Detail of the north-east façade with the dynamic vertical bands of window openings.
6. Detail of the south-west façade with the suspended stainless-steel sun protectors.

7. Inscription »Latvijas Nationālā Bibliotēka« next to the main entrance.
8. Illumination of the north-east façade with the main entrance during the opening ceremony of the National Library.

pp. 30/31
9. The spacious central lobby with the atrium space over it. On the floor polished granite slabs are combined in distinct ethnographic patterns that have been used in the Latvian textiles for centuries.

3

10. The visitors' cloakroom next to the auditorium/ concert hall on the entrance level.
11. The exhibition area on the entrance level.
12. The recreational area as an integral part of the public space on the entrance level.

13. The restaurant at the south-east end of the entrance level with symbolic trees crowning the columns.
14. The bar area in the restaurant.
15. The entrance to the restaurant.

pp. 36/37
16. The auditorium/concert hall with 450 seats, a functional part of the library's conference centre.

13
14
15

16
17
18

17, 18. The impressive atrium, which brings together eight levels of the library, dominates the interior of the building.

pp. 40/41
19. General view of the atrium space from the north-west with stairs linking five levels in the centre.

20. Detail views of the central stairs dividing the atrium into two parts.
21. Functionality, ascetic design and the use of natural materials are inherent qualities of the service area.

pp. 44/45
22. View from the atrium to the central stairs and the reading area with a specially designed bookcase on the right.

IZSTAZU ZĀLE

MŪZIKA • MĀKSLA

23. The top of the bookcase and the public space on level 8.
24. The Interior space of the bookcase with the mirror on the ceiling doubling the real amount of books.

pp. 48/49
25. The sloping glass wall greets the visitor and ensures a permanent presence of books in the public spaces of the library. Behind the sloping glass wall is a huge bookcase rising six storeys high, which is filled with books donated and inscribed by people. It also reflects the composition of the layout – it crowns seven levels of storage space of books and other printed materials totalling to 6.5 million units.

26. The equipment for all reading rooms was produced according to sketches by Gunnar Birkerts.
27. The design of the information desk has a direct reference to the expressive architectural language of the library building.
28. View of the reading area on the north-east side of the building.

29. A recreational zone divides the reading area into two parts.
30. The children's reading area is specially designed and equipped. This is the only room in the library where colours differ from the interplay of silvery grey hues with light-coloured wooden planes.

31. The first section of the atrium is overlooked by peculiarly shaped skylights rising above the facade.
32. View to the skylights and the atrium from the reading rooms of level 8.

pp. 56/57
33. Being a quintessential embodiment of the silvery-grey colour scheme, the spacious atrium provides accessibility to a wide spectrum of the library's functions and offers a spectacular spatial crowning.

34, 35. The spaces of the two-level top of the library are made of metal structures, and wide expanses of glass provide great views across the River Daugava and the historic centre of Riga from a height of 60 m. The top floors of the library are designed for public events, and they include information about the National Library project and Gunnar Birkerts' œuvre.

National Library of Latvia
Mūkusalas iela 3
Riga, LV-1423

Construction period
2008–2014

Commissioner of the design and construction of the building
Ministry of Culture of Latvia in collaboration with the National Library of Latvia

Architect
Gunnar Birkerts, in partnership with the office Arhitektu birojs Ģelzis-Šmits-Arhetips – Modris Ģelzis, Mārcis Mežulis, Sandra Laganovska, Dainis Šmits, and others.

Structural Engineers
LERA, Leslie E. Robertson Associates Structural Engineers and BKB, Būvinženieru konsultāciju birojs

Other engineers
General project management: Constructus. Individual domains: Jensen Consult & Arhis inženieri, N&T Projekts, Constructus, Kārlis, O3FM, FF Signāls, Latcoals, Būvinženieru konsultāciju birojs, E. Daniševska birojs, and Joseph R. Loring and Associates Inc. Consulting Engineers

General contractor
National Builders Association of Latvia including Skonto būve, RBSSKALS, and RE&RE

Management and supervision of the construction process
Hill International N.V.

Technical parameters
Height: 68.3 m, length: 170 m, width: 44 m, total area: 40,455 m^2, building volume: 263,000 m^3, glass façades: 15,300 m^2, stainless-steel roof: 7,400 m^2, granite slab flooring: 3,268 m^2, maple plank flooring: 6,566 m^2, birch wood panelling: 5,370 m^2

Building costs
162.7 million Euro